To

From

Date

The Indescribable Gift

RICHARD EXLEY

ILLUSTRATIONS BY PHIL BOATWRIGHT

New Leaf Press

For information write:
New Leaf Press, Inc.
P.O. Box 726
Green Forest, AR 72638

ISBN: 0-89221-525-9
Library of Congress: 2002105439

Design by D² DesignWorks
Illustrations by Phil Boatwright

Please visit our web site for other great titles:
www.newleafpress.net

Printed in the United States of America.

To the glory of Jesus Christ,
who is both the giver and the gift.

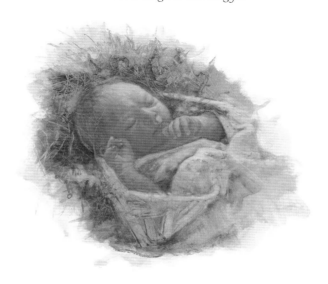

TABLE OF CONTENTS

The Indescribable Gift

The Indescribable Gift gives you the opportunity to experience the birth of Jesus in an intimate way by allowing you to share in the thoughts and feelings of those who were there. Within the factual framework of Scripture, history, and tradition, I give my imagination free reign to create a real life account of this glorious event.

As a knowledgeable reader, you will readily recognize where Scripture ends and imagination begins. Yet, because I have made my creativity congruent with the facts, I believe you will also recognize the reality of this account. What makes these vignettes true to life is not in the incidental "facts" which I have created, but in the reality of their universal humanity. This is how people feel in these kinds of circumstances. And this is why people do these kinds of things.

I have endeavored to make this account true to what we are as human beings. If I have succeeded, it will speak to you in a deeply personal, perhaps even life-changing way.

Instead of just *reading* about the birth of Jesus this Christmas season, *experience* it through the accounts of those who were there.

CHAPTER ONE
Zechariah

With an exaggerated deliberateness,
the old man extracts a small scroll from his bag
and hands it to her.

ZECHARIAH

Ascending one final hill the old man pauses, weary from his journey, to survey the village spread out on the Judean hillside below. Lifting a gnarled hand he shades his eyes against the setting sun, straining to locate his home in the gathering dusk. At last he does, and though he is tired he now quickens his pace, anxious to be home. He has only been gone a little more than a week, but it seems longer. So much has happened.

Turning onto the path leading to his modest dwelling, he catches sight of a stout woman through a small window. Though they have been husband and wife for nearly fifty years, he is now seized by a rush of emotion unlike anything he has ever known. Shedding his weariness like a discarded garment, he hurries into the house. Grabbing the woman about her waist, he crushes her to himself.

Although the fierceness of Zechariah's embrace catches her by surprise, Elizabeth gives herself to it without hesitation. He is slight while she is stout, still he manages to whirl her around the room, so great is his joy. Finally, he collapses in a gasping heap while tears of joy course down his cheeks.

"What has come over you?" she demands in mock anger, her expression a mixture of confusion and joy.

Without thinking Zechariah attempts to speak, but he cannot utter a peep. His lips

"Do not be afraid, Zechariah," the angel said, as though he could read my thoughts. "Your prayer has been heard. Your wife Elizabeth will bear you a son, and you are to give him the name John."

move, but no sound is forthcoming. In an instant Elizabeth's joy turns to concern. She reaches out her hand to touch his thin lips, her eyes full of questions.

Brushing aside her concerns with an impatient wave of his arm, Zechariah leads her to a cushion and motions for her to sit down. Reluctantly she concurs, perching her ample frame anxiously on the edge of the cushion.

With an exaggerated deliberateness the old man extracts a small scroll from his bag and hands it to her. Looking over her shoulder, he watches as she opens it with trembling fingers and begins to read:

My Dearest Elizabeth:

Do not be frightened. Though I cannot speak there is nothing to be alarmed about. It is a sign from God confirming the amazing thing He is about to do. So wonderful is His promise to us that I would gladly be mute all the days of my life rather than forfeit His blessing.

Forgive me. In my excitement I am getting ahead of myself. Let me start at the beginning and I will try to leave nothing out.

You know that as a priest of the order of Abijah I have spent my entire adult life in sacred service. Yet I have never been privileged to burn incense on the golden altar. I am not the only priest who has been denied this sacred honor. With twenty-four priestly orders, there are far more priests than the temple service requires. As a consequence each order only serves in the temple two weeks out of the entire year. Each day a single priest is chosen by lots to offer incense in the holy place. As there are thousands of priests, no priest is allowed to perform this duty more than once in his lifetime. Still, there are those who serve their whole lives without once being chosen.

On the first day of our temple service I was chosen for this holy task and, as you can well imagine, I was profoundly moved. As the appointed hour approached, I felt my heart pounding with the kind of excitement I had not experienced since I was a very young man. The moment for which I had waited a lifetime was finally at hand.

Alone at last in the holy place, I was overcome with a sense of awe. Before me hung the richly embroidered curtain which separated the holy place from the Holy of Holies. Only the High Priest is allowed to enter there, and only once a year on the Day of Atonement. The veil was sixty feet long and thirty feet wide, woven a handbreadth thick of seventy-two plaits with twenty-four threads each. It was resplendent with cherubim woven in scarlet, blue, purple, and gold. To my left stood the table of shewbread, immediately in front of me was the golden altar of incense, and to my right the seven-branched candlestick burned brightly.

As I waited for the signal to burn the incense, my thoughts turned toward you. You are a most godly woman, a fitting wife for a priest, "...upright in the sight of God, observing all the Lord's commandments and regulations blamelessly." Being a descendant of Aaron the first High Priest, I knew you would appreciate the honor that had at last befallen me.

In most ways ours has been a blessed marriage. We share much in common, especially our devotion to the God of Israel. Faithfully we have served Him, and like devout Jews everywhere, we long for the coming of our Messiah. I cherish the many times we talk of this blessed event late into the night. Surely it must be soon.

Thinking about our marriage that day in the Holy of Holies, I felt a familiar ache. Years ago, when we were young, we talked of having a house full of sons. Like many Jewish couples we even dared to hope that we might be privileged to give birth to the Messiah, or at least to one of his ancestors. But as *the years have passed with no children being born to us, that dream died. Still, the disappointment lived on, intruding on my thoughts even in that holy moment.*

At last the signal was given and I turned my thoughts fully to my sacred duties. Like a thousand priests before me and a thousand priests before them, I scattered the incense on the white-hot coals covering the golden altar. In an instant the altar was shrouded in a fragrant smoke that ascended to God. Outside in the temple court, hundreds of worshippers fell face down before the Lord and spread out their hands in silent supplication, their prayers joining with the incense-offering as it rose to God.

I stood motionless before the altar, savoring this once-in-a-lifetime moment to the fullest, nearly overcome with a sense of holiness. Involuntarily I found myself thinking, "Surely the Lord is in this place," and what a wonderfully dreadful thought that was! The sense of His nearness was almost more than I could bear. Like Isaiah of old, I felt undone on the inside, unworthy of being in His presence. Yet, for all of that, I had no desire to flee, no desire to escape His overwhelming nearness.

Though my eyes were tightly closed in silent prayer, I sensed a presence. Turning toward it, I felt a radiance upon my face, and through my closed eyelids I saw a rainbow of colors, something you might see should you stare at the sun with your eyes closed. Gathering my courage I tentatively opened my eyes just a crack, only to discover that I was face to face with an angel!

As Elizabeth reads, her face reflects her feelings. Concern gives way to amazed incredulity, then joyous wonder. The scroll is trembling in her hands as her eyes devour the words.

Clamping my eyes tightly closed, I tried to comprehend what was happening. A splash of dazzling colors danced behind my eyelids. Was I having a vision, I wondered, or was this an angelic visitation? By then I was nearly sick with fear.

"Do not be afraid, Zechariah," the angel said, as though he could read my thoughts. "Your prayer has been heard. Your wife Elizabeth will bear you a son, and you are to give him the name John."

He continued to speak even though it must have been obvious that I was having trouble comprehending his message — not the words, for they were clear enough, but the reality of what he was saying. I remember thinking, "Are we truly going to have a son after all these years, after we have lost all hope of ever having children? Can this be true?"

"He will be a joy and delight to you," the angel continued, "for he will be great in the sight of the Lord. He is never to take wine or other fermented drink, and he will be filled with the Holy Spirit even from birth."

Then he spoke the words that pushed me over the edge: "He will go on before the Lord, in the spirit and power of Elijah, to turn the hearts of the fathers to their children and the disobedient to the wisdom of the righteous — to make ready a people prepared for the Lord."

In that instant I knew that this was not merely the promise of a son, but the promise of the coming Messiah. John — our son — was going to prepare the way for the Messiah, just as Malachi the prophet had said nearly four hundred years ago.

More than anything I wanted to believe that the angel's message was true, but I was afraid too. What if I had misunderstood? What if I had misinterpreted his words, made them more what I wanted them to be than what they really were?

Tentatively I ventured a question: "How can I be sure of this? I am an old man and my wife is well along in years."

Instantly I realized that I had made a mistake. I should have kept my thoughts to myself, for my words offended the angel. It was not his truthfulness that I questioned, nor God's ability to make your barren womb fruitful, but my own ability to accurately comprehend what was happening. I could not be sure if an angel was really speaking to me or if this was all a figment of my imagination. I could not help wondering what it would be like the next day, when all I had left of this experience was the memory. How would I know if it really happened?

Drawing himself up to his full height, the angel declared: "I am Gabriel. I stand in the presence of God, and I have been sent to speak to you and to tell you this good news. And now you will be silent and not able to speak until the day this happens, because you did not believe my words, which will come true at their proper time."

Then he was gone and things returned as they were before he appeared. Numbly I stared at the empty space to the right of the altar, searching in vain for some evidence of his presence. There was nothing, not even a hint. The holy place was empty, except for the last wisps of sweet-smelling smoke that lingered above the golden altar.

From the temple court I heard the murmur of impatient voices. I forced myself to resume my priestly duties. They were waiting for me to appear and pronounce the priestly blessing. Taking a deep breath, I calmed myself. Purposefully I strode onto the steps overlooking the temple court. Raising my hands, I silenced the worshippers and prepared to speak.

The familiar words filled my mind, "The Lord bless you and keep you...," but I could not speak. I was as mute as a post.

For a moment fear overwhelmed me and I fell to my knees trembling. Then I understood. I was not being judged or punished. This was a sign. The angel was real! We were going to have a son, you and I. He would be a prophet like Elijah, yet more than a prophet, for he would prepare the people for the coming of the Messiah.

In an instant I was surrounded by my fellow priests and a host of worshippers. They besieged me with questions, demanding to know what had happened to me. Again I tried to speak, tried to explain what transpired in the holy place, but the words would not come. Try as I might, I could not utter a sound. And once more I was overwhelmed with the joyous conviction that we were the unworthy recipients of a special gift from God.

Gesturing wildly with my hands, I finally made them understand that I had seen a vision. That I could not speak was obvious enough, but there was no way I could explain why, not that it would have *been wise to do so even if I could have. There are some things, some experiences, simply too sacred to share, even with those closest to you.*

There is only one person I dared trust with this holy promise — you — Elizabeth — the love of my life.

Having finished the letter, Elizabeth sits for several minutes in awed silence. At last she takes Zechariah's gnarled hands in hers and looks deeply into his eyes. Twice she attempts to speak, but words fail her. Finally she lifts her hands toward heaven and exclaims, in a voice thick with feeling, "The Lord has done this for me. In these days he has shown his favor and taken away my disgrace among the people."

The sense of the Lord's nearness is almost as overwhelming as it had been in the holy place, and now both the old man and his wife are undone. Clinging to each other, they are seized with fits of laughter and then tears, their spirits soaring with songs of praise for the Holy One of Israel.

After a long while Elizabeth dries her tears and smiles shyly, as a young maiden might. Without a word she leads Zechariah to their bed, now fragrant with the promise of God. Gone are the ghosts of past disappointments, and in their place a tender hope resides. The love they share is gentle, but purposeful. God is with them and His promise becomes a reality in the joy of their intimacy.

CHAPTER TWO

Mary

Her secret was consuming her,

yet she knew she couldn't share it with

her parents, or even Joseph.

MARY

The merchant caravan is winding its way through the hill country south of Jerusalem, accompanied by the creak of saddle leather, the occasional snorting of a camel, and the methodical clumping of hooves. Turning in her saddle, the young woman surveys the countryside. She marvels at the way the sun's lingering light transforms the drab terrain. Just moments ago the barren hills were a dismal blending of sun-bleached brown and dusty gray. Now they have a rustic beauty, a delicate shading of sunlight and shadow.

She feels the lead camel driver's eyes upon her, but is careful not to acknowledge it. Though he is a young man and handsome in a rugged sort of way, she has no interest in him. She has no interest in any man for that matter, except her beloved Joseph, to whom she is betrothed. Thinking of him, her thoughts fall into a familiar rut. What will he think? Will he believe her? Will he understand? These and a host of similar thoughts have tormented her for days.

As if reading her mind, the angel spoke again, "You will be with child and give birth to a son, and you are to give him the name Jesus."

With her destination almost within sight, she is assailed anew with doubts. What does she really hope to accomplish? What makes her think Elizabeth will understand?

Once more she reminds herself of the angel's words, taking what comfort she can in them: "Elizabeth, your relative, is going to have a child in her old age, and she who was said to be barren is in her sixth month."

If that is true, Mary reasons, *then maybe, just maybe, she will believe me when I tell her I am going to be the mother of our Messiah.*

How long has it been now? A week and a half? No, closer to two weeks. She had been alone in the house, the rest of her family were busy elsewhere.

The shout of the lead camel driver interrupts her thoughts. She sees the village spread out below them and realizes they have finally arrived, none too soon either, for the last of the light is fading fast. Exhausted though she is, she cannot help but feel a certain satisfaction. She has made it, and tonight she will sleep in a bed again.

Being only thirteen and a woman, a girl really, though she is betrothed, this is her first journey alone. When she made her desire known, her mother absolutely forbid her to go. "No daughter of mine is going to join a caravan," she declared. "That's the most scandalous thing I've ever heard. What would Joseph think?"

Knowing there was no reasoning with her mother, Mary waited until she could catch her father alone and appealed to him. He took some persuading, but in the end he gave in. If he hadn't, she didn't know what she would have done. Her secret was consuming her, yet she knew she couldn't share it with her parents, or even Joseph. Elizabeth was her only hope.

Seeking out the head merchant, Mary thanks him for his kindness in allowing her to travel with his caravan, then she takes her leave. Shouldering her small bundle of clothing and personal items, she hurries through the nearly dark streets. A vaguely familiar path emerges from the deepening dusk. She ascends it, walking toward the modest dwelling that is her destination.

Nearing the house, her steps slow until she is almost standing still. What madness could have made her think this was a good idea? Painfully she inches her way toward the door, nearly sick with dread. Desperately she tries to think of a reasonable explanation for her sudden appearance, but her mind seems to have forsaken her.

At last she musters her courage and manages a timid knock. While waiting for someone to answer the door, she wrings her hands nervously, half hoping no one is home.

Finally the door opens, and Zechariah stands before her, a candle in one hand. He squints into the darkness. For a moment he studies her face in the flickering light.

He doesn't recognize me, Mary thinks, Not that he should. The last time he saw me I was just a child.

"I'm Mary, from Nazareth," she says, the tremble in her voice betraying her nervousness.

Zechariah still doesn't say anything. Finally Mary thrusts a letter toward him. "It's from my father," she explains. He studies the letter, and then lifts his eyes from the page. He stares at her for a moment more before motioning for her to come in. Without a word he latches the door behind her and turns on his heel. Not knowing what else to do, Mary follows him as he moves toward a distant light.

As they enter the central room, Mary catches sight of Elizabeth bending over the cooking fire. In that instant her fears vanish. Elizabeth is obviously pregnant, just like the angel said. Though her hair is gray with age, being with child has, in many ways, restored her youth. Her eyes sparkle and her face is full of color. There is about her an aura of joyful peace that now floods Mary's soul.

"Elizabeth," she cries, rushing forward to embrace her.

But before Mary can reach her, the Spirit of the Lord comes upon Elizabeth and she begins to prophecy in a loud voice: "Blessed are you among women, and blessed is the child you will bear! But why am I so favored, that the mother of my Lord should come to me? As soon as the sound of your greeting reached my ears, the baby in my womb leaped for joy."

Overcome with emotion, Mary falls to her knees and covers her face. Her mind is racing. Elizabeth's prophetic words have confirmed Gabriel's message, erasing any lingering doubts she might have had. For the first time since that fateful day, she now gives herself fully to the memory.

In an instant she experiences it all again. Once more she is overwhelmed. Well does she remember her initial fear and the angel's assurance. "Do not be afraid, Mary," he said, "you have found favor with God."

Though his words were reassuring, she could remember thinking only of her own sinfulness — not specific sins, but a general feeling of unworthiness. Who was she that the angel of the Lord should visit her? And what was this all about?

As if reading her mind, the angel spoke again, "You will be with child and give birth to a son, and you are to give him the name Jesus. He will be great and will be called the Son of the Most High. The Lord God will give him the throne of his father David, and he will reign over the house of Jacob forever; his kingdom will never end."

His words were familiar to Mary, as they would be to any pious Jew. He was reciting the Messianic prophecy called the "Davidic Covenant" — the same prophetic words heard time and again in the synagogue readings.

What Mary couldn't figure out was how it related to her. Was she to be the earthly mother of the Messiah? Was the only begotten Son of God to enter the world through her womb?

Though not yet married, she knew how babies were conceived. What the angel said simply was not possible. Ever the practical one, she remembered asking, "How will this be since I am a virgin?"

"The Holy Spirit will come upon you," he explained, "and the power of the Most High will overshadow you. The holy one to be born will be called the Son of God."

By then her mind was reeling and all she could think to say was, "I am the Lord's servant. May it be to me as you have said."

As suddenly as the angel appeared he was gone, and Mary was left alone with her jumbled thoughts. She was at once both transfixed and terrified. The honor that every Jewish woman dreamed of was to be hers. Yet the circumstances under which it was to occur were not those any pious woman would choose. Whatever honor there might be in giving birth to the Messiah would surely be lost in the ensuing scandal when it was discovered that his mother was an unmarried woman.

And what of her marriage to Joseph? Would that devout man still want her once he learned that she was with child, or would he divorce her?

Well did she know the seriousness of her situation. Jewish law considered the violation of the fidelity of a betrothed person adultery. Under the law, it was punishable by death. She did not think that would happen, because the Romans reserved the right of capital punishment to themselves. Still, living without Joseph might prove to be a punishment worse than death.

Now, all these concerns and any others Mary might have had are washed away in this holy moment. Joyously she thinks, Elizabeth knows! She understands what has happened to me. I was right to come here.

Then the spirit of prophecy falls upon Mary and she lifts her voice in prophetic song. Although the words are familiar, coming as they do from the Old Testament, the Holy Spirit now enlarges their meaning.

> "My soul glorifies the Lord
> and my spirit rejoices in God my Savior,
> for he has been mindful
> of the humble state of his servant.
> From now on all generations will call me blessed,
> for the Mighty One has done great things for me —
> holy is his name.
> His mercy extends to those who fear him,
> from generation to generation.
> He has performed mighty deeds with his arm;
> he has scattered those who are proud
> in their inmost thoughts.
> He has brought down rulers from their thrones
> but has lifted up the humble.
> He has filled the hungry with good things,
> but has sent the rich away empty.
> He has helped his servant Israel,
> remembering to be merciful

to Abraham and his descendants forever,
even as he said to our fathers."

Finishing, Mary collapses into Elizabeth's arms, overcome with the sense of God's nearness. What a pair we make, she thinks. We would seem to have nothing in common. I am hardly more than a child while she is old enough to be my grandmother. Yet God has joined our spirits and the destiny of the sons we now carry in our wombs.

How marvelous it is that the Spirit should reveal my pregnancy to Elizabeth even before it is obvious to me. Now I know, beyond all doubt, that this is the Lord's doing. Though it may not be easy, I know He will be with me. With His help I will give birth to the Savior.

Holding Mary at arm's length, Elizabeth says, "Let me look at you child."

For a long time they stand there, staring into one another's eyes. From across the room Zechariah watches, nearly overcome as there passes between them feelings too deep for words. Finally Elizabeth breaks away and busies herself preparing a simple meal. When she does, Zechariah shuffles across the room and hands Mary a tablet upon which he has recorded the words of Elizabeth's prophetic greeting and her own song of praise.

Hugging the tablet to her heart, Mary blinks hard to hold back her tears. "Thank you Zechariah," she says.

Reading the prophecy, she determines to commit the words to memory. Such profound truths cannot be trusted to something as fragile as a tablet. Somehow she seems to know that in the difficult days ahead they will prove to be a source of strength and comfort to her.

CHAPTER THREE

Elizabeth

Long ago Zechariah and Elizabeth had ceased
talking about children of their own, though for a time they
each continued to pray in secret for a child.

ELIZABETH

At last the house is quiet. Exhausted from her journey and the ensuing excitement, Mary is already asleep. Zechariah has retired for the night as well, leaving Elizabeth with a few minutes of solitude. Once the eating utensils are washed and put away, she finds her favorite stool and sits down to reflect on the day. The memory of her joyous encounter with Mary continues to echo within her soul. Unconsciously she rubs her belly, where her baby now rests peacefully.

A slow smile spreads across her wrinkled features as she recalls how he leaped within her womb at the sound of Mary's greeting. He is an active baby, she muses, and I have spent hours enjoying his restlessness within my womb, but what happened today was unlike anything I have ever experienced. Somehow he must have recognized the presence of his Lord and leaped for joy.

How mysterious are the ways of the Spirit!

Once more joy floods her soul and she sinks to her knees in grateful worship. Not only has she been given a son in her old age, but she is now privileged to minister unto the mother of her Lord as well. Lifting her hands toward heaven, she praises God saying, "The Lord has done this for me. In these days he has shown his favor and taken away my disgrace among the people."

Her joy is all the sweeter because of the sorrow she has known. In Israel there is nothing

Once the eating utensils are washed and put away, she finds her favorite stool and sits down to reflect on the day.

worse than being a barren woman, and she was barren for more than fifty years. When it first became apparent that she was not going to conceive, she was nearly consumed with grief. It settled upon her like the angel of death and would not let her go. In those days her laughter dried up and she seemed to age visibly from one day to the next.

Each month, as the time of her menstruation drew near, she fell into a black depression. Though Zechariah assured her that he did not love her any less because she could not bear him children, she took no comfort in that fact. In truth, it was not Zechariah's displeasure she feared, but her own. In her heart, Elizabeth despised herself.

To a Jewish woman, nothing was more fundamental than bearing children, and at this crucial task she was a complete failure. She could not have felt more crippled if she had been born maimed. Truly, a crippled limb would have been easier to bear.

Not infrequently her self-loathing turned into anger. On more than one occasion she lashed out at Zechariah until that good man was nearly beside himself. Like Rachel she cried, "Give me children, or I'll die." And like Rachel's husband Jacob, Zechariah grew angry in his helplessness. More than once the neighbors heard him scream, "Am I God that I can give you children?"

At other times Elizabeth blamed God. She could never admit such a thing, not even to herself, but it was true. Mostly though, she blamed herself. She could only conclude that the Almighty was punishing her, though for what she could not imagine. Since childhood she had feared God, observing all His commandments and regulations blamelessly.

Elizabeth vacillated between abject despair and desperate hope. Obsessively she relived the Old Testament stories of the great women of faith: Sarah, Rebekah, Rachel, and Hannah.

They were barren, each and every one of them — until God intervened. They became her secret sisters. From their experiences she drew strength to sustain her failing hopes.

Secretly she wept before the Lord and poured out the misery of her soul. Like Hannah she prayed, "O Lord Almighty, if you will only look upon your servant's misery and remember me, and not forget your servant but give her a son, then I will give him to the Lord for all the days of his life, and no razor will ever be used on his head."

Unlike those holy women of old, however, her prayers were not answered. For Elizabeth there was no divine reversal, no supernatural intervention, no opening of her barren womb. Month after month, year after year, she experienced the same devastating disappointment, until at last her hopes withered and died.

For a time it seemed she might become a bitter woman, but in the end she was able to right herself. Through it all Zechariah was a tower of strength. Not once did he blame her, not even when she succumbed to her black moods.

Finally Elizabeth made peace with her pain. It was not easy, but what choice did she have? If she was to ever enjoy life, she had to accept her condition. Ultimately she chose gratefulness over grief. Instead of lamenting the fact that she was childless, she chose to thank God for all the ways He had blessed her union with Zechariah.

Yes, Elizabeth was childless, but she was not desolate. The God of Israel was her strength, a great help in time of trouble. She told all who would listen, she was blessed with a godly husband, a priest. Not only did they share their faith, but many other things as well. Hard though it was, she turned her maternal love on the children in their extended family. As a result, she became the favorite aunt for a host of nieces and nephews.

Still, nothing she did could long remove the ache caused by her childlessness. Content though she was, there would always be an empty place in her heart, a place that could only be filled by a child of her own.

Long ago Zechariah and Elizabeth had ceased talking about children of their own, though for a time they each continued to pray in secret for a child. Then they stopped even that. Moving into mid-life and beyond, their thoughts turned toward other things.

But God had not forgotten their prayers, and in the course of time He sent the angel Gabriel to Zechariah with a message: "Your prayer has been heard. Your wife Elizabeth will bear you a son, and you are to give him the name John."

When Zechariah tried to tell Elizabeth what had happened, he couldn't speak. Although his lips moved he couldn't make a sound. For a moment Elizabeth was sick with fear, thinking he might have suffered a stroke. Then, like a flash, she remembered the story of Hannah.

In the agony of her barrenness, Hannah prayed and "her lips were moving but her voice was not heard." But God heard her inaudible intercession and in the course of time Hannah conceived and gave birth to a son. She named him Samuel, saying, "Because I asked the Lord for him."

Could it be, Elizabeth had wondered, *that after all these years I am going to be blessed with a son? After all this time, after finally coming to terms with my infertility, I am going to be given a child?*

She had been afraid to believe, afraid to even consider the possibility. Another disappointment was simply more than she could bear. Yet, against her better judgment, she found her hopes soaring. Somehow she knew God was going to give her a son, even before Zechariah handed her the scroll explaining what had happened to him.

The baby now stirs within her womb and she rejoices again at the faithfulness of God. How appropriate, she decides, that the angel should tell us to name him John, which according to Hebrew etymology, means "the gracious gift of God."

Like expectant mothers the world over, she gives herself to speculation concerning the child who now sleeps in her womb. *Will he look like me,* she wonders, *or will he favor Zechariah? And what of his temperament? Will he be a playful child, or will there be about him an extraordinary seriousness befitting his call in life?*

These and a thousand similar thoughts have occupied her mind these past months. At last, with Mary's coming, she has someone with whom to share her thoughts, someone who will understand her hopes and dreams. Even as Mary cannot disclose to anyone that the child she carries is the Messiah, neither can Elizabeth tell anyone that her son is the forerunner, the one who will prepare the way for the coming of the Lord.

As Elizabeth considers these things, a horde of fresh questions fill her mind. How did Mary know she was pregnant? For five months she did not tell a soul. Who would have believed her? She had remained in seclusion, waiting until her condition was so obvious no one could doubt what the Lord had done for her. Yet, Mary seemed to know. Why else would she risk such a dangerous journey from Nazareth?

And of Mary's situation, Elizabeth knew nothing beyond what the Spirit revealed to her today. She wonders if Mary is married. According to the last word they had received, she was betrothed to a man named Joseph, a carpenter. How unusual that the Messiah should be born to a peasant carpenter and a simple village girl. Then she remembered something about royalty in Joseph's family tree. Tomorrow she must ask Mary when she first realized she was going to be the mother of the Messiah. I will insist that she tell me everything, she thinks. She must leave nothing out. Did the angel of the Lord visit her, I wonder, as he did Zechariah? Or did the Lord speak to her in a different, but equally supernatural way?

Though Elizabeth is excited beyond words, she is also tired. With an effort she now hoists herself up and makes her way toward her bed. Tomorrow, Mary and I will talk as only sisters can, for by virtue of God's favor we have become sisters of the heart. To whom but me can she speak of the marvelous things the Lord has done for her? And though I have Zechariah, my situation is not unlike hers. No one but Mary can fully appreciate what God has done for me.

CHAPTER FOUR
The Return

Picking up her small bundle,

Mary pauses at the door and surveys the small room one final time.

It has been home to her these past three months.

THE RETURN

The sun is streaming through the window, laying broad swaths of warm light across the worn floor. Mary checks the tightly rolled bundle that contains her meager possessions one final time. Satisfied, she places it near the door. Soon, she thinks, Zechariah will come for me. Together we will walk to the market place, where I will join a caravan of merchants for my journey back to Nazareth.

For a moment tears swim in her eyes, and she is nearly overcome with emotion at the thought of leaving. During the past three months she has grown close to Elizabeth and Zechariah, closer than she has ever been to anyone. Though Elizabeth is old enough to be her grandmother, she has been like a beloved sister to her. They have become intimates, sharing secrets they could never tell anyone else.

He will not look at her, and try as she might, she cannot think of anything to ease the hurt her words have caused him.

Elizabeth never makes her feel foolish, regardless of how silly her questions might be. Nor did she bat an eye when Mary told her that she was still a virgin. Not once did she question her truthfulness.

She must have mentioned it to Zechariah though, because the next day he went to the synagogue and returned with a small piece of parchment on which he had written a passage from the prophet Isaiah. Taking it from him, Mary began to read: "Therefore the Lord himself will give you a sign: The virgin will be with child and will give birth to a son and will call him Immanuel."

At the sight of those words, Mary's heart raced. Jumping to her feet, she grabbed the scroll and rushed to show it to Elizabeth. Breathlessly she said, "Here is proof, not only of my purity, but of the deity of my child as well, for Immanuel means "God with us."

Looking at Elizabeth for reassurance she said, "Surely no one will question me now."

"Those who choose to believe," Elizabeth replied solemnly, "will not need proof. For those who don't, there will never be proof enough."

Mary was puzzled by her words then, as she is now these many weeks later. In spite of her questions, Elizabeth had steadfastly refused to explain herself. Of course, Mary reasons, the idea of a virgin conceiving a child seems ludicrous. But in light of Isaiah's prophecy, how could anyone doubt it, especially when they learn of my encounter with the angel Gabriel?

Reaching into a hidden pocket in the inner folds of her garment, Mary fingers a well-worn scroll. It has become a sort of talisman for her. On it is written a copy of the letter Zechariah gave to Elizabeth, plus the transcription he made of Elizabeth's prophecy the night Mary arrived.

Armed with these, Mary is anxious to return to Nazareth and share her secret with Joseph. She told Elizabeth, "I know it won't be easy, but I do believe God has used my time with you to prepare me. Surely He has been preparing Joseph's heart as well."

"Mary," Elizabeth calls from the front of the house, "it is time to go. Zechariah is waiting."

Picking up her small bundle, Mary pauses at the door and surveys the small room one final time. It has been home to her these past three months. Although it is plain, containing only a bed and a small stand with a wash basin and a pitcher of water, it is special to her. Many a night she stood at the narrow window, studying the wide sky while contemplating the words of the angel: "The Holy Spirit will come upon you, and the power of the Most High will overshadow you. So the holy one to be born will be called the Son of God."

No matter how many times she relives that experience, it never loses its wonder. Time and again she asks herself, "Who am I that I should be the mother of the only begotten son of God? I am only a peasant girl."

On more than one occasion she discussed her feelings with Elizabeth. "Auntie," she asked, "why do you suppose God chose me to be the mother of our Lord?"

"You were chosen," Elizabeth replied, "because of your ordinariness, not in spite of it. God has been doing that sort of thing for generations."

Mary's reminiscing is cut short when Elizabeth calls a second time. "What's keeping you child? Zechariah is waiting."

Hurrying toward the front of the house, Mary braces herself. Leaving Elizabeth will not be easy, but she is determined not to make a scene. Still, she cannot help herself. At the sight of that dear woman she bursts into tears. Dropping her bundle she throws herself into Elizabeth's arms, who is now huge with child. Feeling her heavy belly hard against her own stomach, Mary thinks, Soon I will be like that. As always, she draws strength from Elizabeth's presence.

Hugging Mary tightly, Elizabeth speaks softly into her ear. "Blessed are you among women, and blessed is the child you will bear!"

There is something about the way she says it that is more sobering than reassuring. Sensing the subtle nuances in her voice, Mary asks, "Elizabeth, are you trying to tell me something?"

"Nothing that you don't already know," she replies. "God's chosen people have always had a hard road. You will be no different. You are special and being special is never easy."

By now Elizabeth's eyes are tearing up and her voice is husky. "If things don't work out with Joseph," she says, "you can always come and stay with us."

Not trusting herself to speak, Mary simply nods while swallowing hard. Handing her bundle to her, Elizabeth gently pushes her toward the door. Zechariah is waiting beside the road and Mary hurries toward him, not daring to look back. Nearing the bottom of the hill she risks a backward glance, then a final wave after catching sight of Elizabeth staring after them.

When they reach the market place, Zechariah negotiates her passage and entrusts her to the care of a respected merchant who is traveling to Nazareth. In short order the caravan moves out, and Mary finds herself falling into the familiar routine. Soon the monotony of the trail lulls her into a lethargic torpor, and she passes the next five days lost in her own thoughts. It is only as they near Nazareth that she rouses herself.

As the dusty caravan enters the familiar streets of her village, the sun is laying long shadows across the market place. Her father is waiting, and after giving her a warm embrace he studies her at length. His eyes are full of questions, but he respects Mary's privacy too much to venture a question.

"I love you, Abba Father," Mary says, giving his work hardened hand a tender squeeze.

Seeing that Mary is not inclined to discuss her trip he takes her arm saying, "We must hurry home. It is nearly time for the Sabbath to begin."

Entering the humble dwelling that has been her home since birth, Mary is hit with a wave of nostalgia, a host of childhood memories nearly overwhelming her. The familiar smell of the ritual Sabbath meal, modest though it is, now seems exotic. The murmur of voices from the other room, punctuated from time to time by soft laughter, is like music to her ears. Unconsciously, she identifies the voice of each family member.

For the first time she realizes that she is homesick, that she has desperately missed her family. We have been separated, she thinks, not only by time and distance, but by the secret I carry in my heart.

In that moment Mary is struck again by the wisdom of Elizabeth. How many times did she tell me secrets separate? More than I can remember. At last I understand. It is not only information that we withhold, but a part of ourselves.

Pausing in the doorway, Mary considers her own situation. By withholding the most important event in my life, she muses, I have distanced myself from those I love. Though I share their name I no longer feel like I belong. Even if they don't sense it, I do. In truth, I feel like a stranger within my own family, but soon all of that will change. Once I tell Joseph, I will let the whole family in on the news. Then everyone can share my joy.

Following the Sabbath meal the family adjourns to the synagogue for the Sabbath service. Though men and women are required to sit in different sections, separated from each other by a screen, Mary catches sight of Joseph as he enters. He is a tall man, and slim, with hands hardened from working in his carpenter shop. There is a gentleness about him that belies his strength, and a steadfastness beyond his years. They have been betrothed for nearly a year, still Mary does not know him well enough to say that she loves him. She is sure, though, that one day she will.

Tonight she cannot concentrate on the reading of Scripture or the chanting of the ancient Psalms, beautiful though they are. Instead, her mind is filled with a horde of conflicting thoughts as she considers possible ways to break the news to Joseph. None of them seem right, and she is still debating with herself when the service ends.

Once they are outside the synagogue, Joseph makes his way toward Mary as she stands with her family. He greets her father and mother before turning to her. Clearing his throat he inquires about her health and then asks if they might speak privately. Of course, he does not mean they will be alone, for that is improper, and Joseph is of all men most conscious of propriety. He is simply asking her to separate herself a few feet from her family, so they can talk without being overheard.

Before he can utter a word she says, "Joseph, I have something to tell you. I simply cannot bear to keep it from you any longer. Still, I am afraid of what you might do."

She pauses, waiting for him to say something, anything. When he doesn't she plunges ahead. "I know that what I am about to tell you will be hard to believe, but you must trust me."

Still Joseph does not speak, but his face is flushed and in his throat his pulse is racing.

Taking a deep breath, Mary continues in a voice Joseph has to lean toward her to hear. "Although I have never known a man," she says, "I am with child. The baby I am carrying does not belong to an earthly father, but was placed in my womb by the Holy Spirit."

There is more that she would like to say, but the look on Joseph's face stops her cold.

Shocked disbelief turns his dark features a sickly gray, then sorrow clouds his eyes. He looks at her, his eyes filling with hurt that slowly gives way to anger.

In desperation Mary tries to explain. "Joseph, it's not what you think. This is the Lord's doing. I'm going to be the mother of our Messiah."

"How can you even suggest such a thing?" he asks, his words bitter and biting. "It's bad enough that you should betray me and nullify the promises our families have made, but how dare you risk blasphemy by concocting such a story."

He will not look at her, and try as she might, she cannot think of anything to ease the hurt her words have caused him. Though she carries in the folds of her garment the transcription of Elizabeth's prophecy and a copy of Zechariah's letter, there is no reason to reveal them now. Like Elizabeth said, "Those who choose to believe do not need proof. For those who don't, there will never be proof enough."

"Joseph please," she pleads, but to no avail.

Without a backward glance he stalks into the night, trailing sorrow and anger behind him. She is tempted to run after him and try to force him to listen to reason, but custom does not allow it. Though they are engaged they cannot be alone until it is time to consummate the marriage. Until then, they can only converse within the sight of others.

Even if she dared to run after him what could she say? How could she make him believe that she is pregnant by an act of God? Such an explanation sounds foolish even to her own ears.

After watching Joseph disappear into the night, she rejoins her family. "What was that all about?" her mother asks. "It's not like Joseph to leave in a huff."

Feigning ignorance, she replies, "Was he in a huff? I didn't notice."

Letting it drop, her mother continues to study Mary out of the corner of her eye. Something is going on, she thinks, of that I am sure. Let Mary act innocent if she will, she has not heard the last of this. I am her mother and I know something is bothering her.

Silently they trudge home, Mary trailing a little behind, her heart nearly breaking. How naive her earlier optimism now seems in light of Joseph's reaction. What ever possessed her to think that anyone would believe her? Indeed, it is probably just a matter of time until Joseph divorces her and then her name will become a by-word in Nazareth.

That night she keeps her own counsel. Carefully she locks her tears and her fears in her heart. She speaks to no one — not even to her father or mother. Around her, her brothers and sisters sleep huddled close against the cold, while she keeps her lonely vigil. She has done all she can do. Now the future is up to God.

CHAPTER FIVE

Joseph

As Joseph speaks,

Mary's face comes alive, dispelling his fears.

J O S E P H

Leaving Mary, Joseph stumbles blindly into the night. For hours he wanders the dark streets of Nazareth. His restless walking takes him well beyond the limits of the law, that which is referred to as a "Sabbath day's journey." Never has he violated the Sabbath, never until tonight. Now it seems he cannot help himself. Mary's devastating disclosure has left him stunned, and he cannot be still. If the truth be known, he is shaken to the very core of his being. If Mary is capable of something like this, if she cannot be trusted, then who can be? Once more he replays her words in his mind: "I am with child."

When first she spoke them he could not grasp their meaning. It was simply unthinkable. Never in his wildest imagination would he have thought his sweet Mary capable of such a thing. To him, she was the paragon of virtue, the last person in the world who would be guilty of adultery.

Now her words hammer at him with killing blows, and his imagination is a sadistic ogre. Although he has never so much as touched Mary's hand, he now imagines her in the arms of her secret lover. In his mind's eye he sees her sharing her kisses with him, giving that rogue all the love she had pledged to him. It is more than he can bear, and with a Herculean effort he forces the images from his mind. But he cannot rid himself of the awful pain that eats at his heart.

Turning down a narrow street, he stumbles through the darkness, seeking for an answer, an explanation.

Turning down a narrow street, he stumbles through the darkness, seeking for an answer, an explanation. How could he have made such a mistake? Of Mary's piety he has no doubt. Her's was a devout family, with never a hint of impropriety. From all his observations she seemed to possess the qualities of an ideal wife. Was it all a facade? Was she just waiting for an opportunity before revealing her true character?

Nagging at the edge of his mind is her explanation — "I have never known a man. The baby I am carrying does not belong to an earthly father, but was placed in my womb by the Holy Spirit."

He thrusts it from his mind, anger replacing the hurt that lays like a dead weight in his belly. Does she think him an idiot that he should believe such a tale? He knows how babies are made, and it is not the work of the Holy Spirit!

Now he is consumed with an impotent rage. If he knew who the man was, he would tear him limb from limb. But what good would that do? It would not undo what was done. It would not restore Mary's chastity, nor make her a virgin again.

In an instant he rails at her father. If he had not let her go to Hebron then none of this would have happened. What kind of father would trust his virgin daughter to the company of a caravan of merchants for a five-day journey? What kind of parent would allow his betrothed daughter to live unchaperoned among kin in a distant village?

Having exhausted his anger, he discovers that he feels no better. Neither affixing blame or venting his feelings nor even his bitter tears can change what is done. Mary has broken her pledge of fidelity. She has betrayed his love, desecrated their marriage, and she now carries in her womb the bastard child of her illicit affair.

Yet, even as he rages in his helplessness and grief, a part of his heart yearns for her —

not for the adulterous Mary who has shamed herself and all those who love her, but for that pure, sweet girl who pledged her love and fidelity to him.

Can it be that just hours ago he was a happy man looking forward to seeing his espoused wife after an absence of three months? That man was anxious to tell his beloved about the room he had built on his father's house, the room that was to be their own. That man could hardly wait to share with her his dreams for their future. That man had planned to show her the furniture he had built for them with his own hands, love molding every piece.

But that man is no more. He was put to death by the killing words of the one he loved. In his place is the man he has become — a distraught creature who wanders the dark streets blind with grief. He is a broken thing, like the promises she made but didn't keep. He is just a shell, empty on the inside, as empty as the dreams he once had for their future.

All night long he walks aimlessly through Nazareth's narrow streets, driven by a pain he has never known. Finally exhaustion overtakes him and he turns toward home. Day is just a faint hint on the eastern horizon when he slips into his father's house, being careful not to make a sound. Although he knows his parents will learn of Mary's condition soon enough, he is not ready to face their questions.

The sun is bright when he finally awakes several hours later. For a moment, all is right with the world. From the other room he hears the murmur of voices, outside his window children are playing, and in the distance a dog barks. From years of habit he mumbles sleepily, "This is the day the Lord has made; let us rejoice and be glad in it."

As he stretches a sense of foreboding settles upon him, nothing definite, just a dampening of his enthusiasm. Then he remembers, and a cloud passes across the face of the sun casting a dark shadow over his world. Burying his face in his hands, he sits there fighting back tears as the devastating memory sweeps over him.

Desperately he longs for the sweet oblivion of sleep, but he resists the temptation. Instead he rouses himself, and after splashing cold water over his face, he dresses and prepares for the day. Donning his public face, he goes to join his parents. He must not let them know anything is wrong. Not yet. Not until he has figured out what he is going to do.

The next few days pass in a daze. Like a sleepwalker Joseph greets customers, fills orders, and works in the carpenter shop. All the while his mind is in a turmoil. What he must do is obvious enough, but he cannot bring himself to do it. Although Mary has played him for a fool, he cannot find it in his heart to hurt her. Though she has betrayed his love, he still loves her. Yet, he cannot go through with the marriage either, knowing she carries in her womb a child fathered by another man.

Carefully he considers his options. In Jewish marriage there are three steps. The first step is the engagement, a contract arranged by family members. The second step is the betrothal, a public ratification of the engagement. During this period the couple is considered husband and wife, though the marriage has not been consummated. The only way a betrothal can be terminated is by death or divorce. A young woman whose fiancé dies during this period is called "a virgin who is a widow." The third stage is the marriage proper, when the groom takes his bride into the bridal chamber and consummates the marriage. This is followed by a wedding party.

According to Jewish custom, he can divorce Mary, either publicly before a court or privately with no more than two witnesses. All that is required for a private divorce is the writing of the divorce certificate at the synagogue. Although this is hardly satisfactory, Joseph deems it the best option given the circumstances. It will enable him to spare Mary as much humiliation as possible.

Private though the divorce might be, she will not be spared public disgrace, nor will her family. Nazareth is a small town, and it will not take long for word to get around. Ultimately, she will be expelled from the community and forced to care for her child alone. The thought that she might end up like other women in her circumstance is almost more than Joseph can bear. Most of them either sell themselves into slavery or become prostitutes in order to support themselves.

With everything that is within him he longs to accept Mary's bizarre explanation at face value, but he doesn't know how he can. No matter how much he wants to believe in her purity, reason tells him a virgin does not become pregnant. And, in a case like this, the Scriptures are clear: "If a man happens to meet in a town a virgin pledged to be married and he sleeps with her, you shall take both of them to the gate of that town and stone them to death — the girl because she was in a town and did not scream for help, and the man because he violated another man's wife. You must purge the evil from among you."

After days and nights of painful soul-searching, Joseph at last decides to divorce Mary privately. He will arrange for two witnesses to meet him at the synagogue. Once the divorce document is prepared, he will deliver it to Mary and her father. Hopefully, when that is done he will be able to put this unfortunate mess behind him. Of one thing he is sure, it will be a long time before he considers marriage again.

Collapsing in bed, he cries out to God, "O Lord, give me the strength to do that which is right in Your sight." Having committed his future into the hands of the Lord, he now falls into a deep sleep.

Early the next morning he makes his way toward the house of Mary's father. Though he slept well and awoke confident, this morning's business weighs heavily upon his mind. Will Mary understand, he wonders, or will she hold his actions against him? These and a host of similar thoughts plague him as he nears her father's house.

Now his steps slow involuntarily. His mouth is dry. Tension knots his stomach, forcing him to take several deep breaths in an unsuccessful attempt to calm himself. Finally, he knocks on the door. After what seems an eternity, it is opened by Mary's father. He asks to speak with Mary.

Inviting him in, her father goes to call her. Nervously, Joseph studies the room, which is almost austere in its simplicity. That Mary comes from humble circumstances is readily apparent, but then so does he. His father's house is equally modest.

Mary coughs discreetly, calling him from his thoughts. Her father is standing just beyond the door, clearly visible as custom dictates, but not intruding. As she steps into the room, a shaft of sunlight back-lights her dark hair, creating a halo effect. Though her face is in the shadow, Joseph cannot help but notice that she is unnaturally pale, making her wide eyes seem abnormally large. There is about her an air of calm resignation and a certain sadness.

When at last he speaks, his voice falters. "Mary," he begins hesitantly, "I have been doing a lot of thinking these last few days, and last night I was finally able to reach a decision. I hope you believe me when I tell you that the last thing I would ever do is hurt you."

He lifts his eyes and risks a look at Mary. What he sees nearly tears his heart out of him. Though she is trying to be brave, her lower lip trembles and silent tears leave wet tracks down her pale cheeks. Her stricken look pierces him to the quick and he wonders anew how he could have ever doubted her.

More than anything, he longs to take her in his arms, but he dares not. Gathering his courage he plunges ahead. "Last night the most amazing thing happened. An angel of the Lord came to me in a dream."

"'Joseph, son of David,'" he said, "'do not be afraid to take Mary home as your wife, because what is conceived in her is from the Holy Spirit.'"

As Joseph speaks, Mary's face comes alive, dispelling his fears. There is no mistaking the thankfulness in her eyes. There is no hurt there now, no fear, just joy.

"Then," he tells her, "the angel told me the most amazing thing."

"Yes," she says.

"He said you will give birth to a son, and I am to give him the name Jesus, because he will save his people from their sins."

Reaching inside the folds of her garment, Mary lays hold of the worn parchment. Tears of joy are streaming down her cheeks as she walks across the room and hands it to Joseph. Not being an accomplished reader, he struggles with the words: "Therefore the Lord himself will give you a sign: The virgin will be with child and will give birth to a son, and will call him Immanuel."

"Does this say what I think it says?" Joseph asks in disbelief.

"It does. Zechariah copied it for me. It comes from the prophet Isaiah."

Then she adds, "Although I have never known a man, I am with child. The baby I am carrying does not belong to an earthly father, but was placed in my womb by the Holy Spirit. This is the Lord's doing. I'm going to be the mother of our Messiah."

The very words, that upon first hearing devastated him, now thrill him beyond belief. His sweet Mary is a virgin. She has not betrayed his love, nor violated the promises they made.

Falling to his knees he implores her, "Can you ever forgive me for doubting your chastity?"

"Hush," she says, "hush."

"Mary," he asks, "will you come home with me today and live as my wife. I know we cannot consummate our marriage until after Jesus is born, but in every other way we will be husband and wife."

After making him wait for what seems forever, Mary finally replies. "First we must explain the situation to my parents. Then, if my father agrees, I will be most honored to go home with you as your wife."

Joseph's heart is singing as he goes with Mary to speak with her father. Later they will have to deal with the rumors and innuendoes, but for now they are joyously content. Though there is much he does not understand, of one thing he is sure—God Himself will take care of them.

CHAPTER SIX
The Innkeeper

Turning to the young couple, he says,

"There's a sheep shed in back of the Inn. It's not much, I'll grant you,

but it will shelter you from the cold."

THE INNKEEPER

The long day is finally over, every available sleeping space filled, and Jacob is only too happy to retire to the small quarters he shares with his wife. Closing the door he collapses on his favorite cushion. "Hannah," he calls out, "bring me a basin of water for my tired feet — and make it warm."

While waiting to soak his feet, Jacob takes the day's receipts from the bag he carries carefully concealed at his waist. It has been a good day and the bag is heavy. Dumping the coins in his lap, he runs them through his stubby fingers, taking pleasure in calculating the day's profits.

Finally Hannah arrives with his water, and he heaves a sign of pleasure as he immerses his swollen feet in its steamy warmth. "Thank you, thank you," he says, patting her on the arm. "Come, sit with me. Let's talk."

Desperately, Jacob tries to think of something, anything, to rid himself of this persistent young man.

Opening the ledgers he shows her page after page of figures. "We aren't going to get rich, Hannah," he confides, "but we should be able to spend our last years in a degree of comfort, thanks to recent events."

That she is uncomfortable with his obsession with figures is obvious, still she manages a small smile. Things could be worse, she reasons. I could be married to a less astute man, or even a shepherd. Nonetheless she is bothered. To her way of thinking, it is wrong to make a profit from another's misfortune, especially one of your own countrymen.

Such concerns are foreign to Jacob, and already he is calculating ways to take further advantage of the situation. With pleasure he recalls how this good fortune came about. It began several months back with a Roman decree issued by Caesar Augustus, the nephew of Julius Caesar and arguably the most powerful of the Caesars. With imperial arrogance he decreed that everyone return to their city of origin for an official census. It was an outrageous order, creating unspeakable hardships for thousands of families. Many would have to travel for days, some even weeks, in order to register.

When the decree was posted in Bethlehem it attracted a crowd, many of whom could not read. Being better educated than most, Jacob pushed through the throng and read the proclamation in a commanding voice. At first there was only stunned silence as each man contemplated its impact on his own life. Finally someone cursed Caesar, and in an instant the street was filled with an ugly undercurrent of thinly disguised resentment.

Jacob slipped away, and just in time too. Hardly had he reached the inn before the clatter of hooves filled the street. Stepping to the door, he saw a Roman chariot bearing down on the angry townspeople. Belatedly they realized their peril and scattered like a covey of startled quail. A few stragglers felt the bite of the captain's whip and one old man was knocked sprawling, but for the most part it was just another day in the life of Bethlehem's oppressed people.

There was a lot of muttering and some angry talk for a few days, but nothing ever came of it. Such was life with the Roman heel on your neck. What could they do? Being mostly shepherds and shopkeepers, they were no match for the legions of Rome. So they learned to hate and to dream of the day when the Messiah would come and put their enemies to flight. Then the despised Romans would be the tail and not the head. Then they would have their revenge.

Jacob had been outraged too, on principle mostly, because the decree created no real hardship for him. Bethlehem of Judea was the city of his birth, and he could register for the census right here. If the truth be known, he had spent all of his life in this obscure place. His father was here before him, and his father's father was here before him, and his father's father before him — on back as far as anyone could remember. As long, he guessed, as there had been a Bethlehem of Judea, his family had been here.

As his outrage subsided he began to see things in a different light. This time the hated Romans had done him a favor, not deliberately mind you, but a favor nonetheless. Caesar Augustus' decree would prove to be a blessing in disguise. With the foresight that his family was known for, Jacob enlarged the Inn in order to accommodate the anticipated influx of people. Nothing elaborate, just one large room where weary travelers could sleep out of the cold. Nothing more. Cheapest construction possible.

The travelers came too, just like he knew they would. What choice did they have? And they were about what he expected — bitter and complaining, angry for the most part, resentful of this disruption to their lives and looking for someone to take their frustration out on.

Who better to take it out on, he thinks, with a weary grimace, than this hard-hearted skinflint of an innkeeper? They curse him, shake their fists in his face, and accuse him of taking advantage of their situation. In the end they grudgingly fork over their money and make their way to their cramped quarters for the night.

I haven't increased my prices, he thinks, not really. Of course I raised them a bit, but not exorbitantly. I'm certainly not trying to gouge anyone. It's just good business — the old law of supply and demand. Any good businessman would do the same.

A loud banging on the outer door jerks him from his brief reprieve. Every sleeping space is filled, so he ignores it and continues to run a pile of coins through his callused fingers, dreaming of easier days in the not-too-distant future.

The banging grows more insistent and he shouts, "Go away. There's no room in the inn."

Still the knocking persists, so he reluctantly hoists himself to his feet and shuffles to the door. Opening it just a crack, he sees an exhausted young man and, in the shadows behind him, a young woman slumped on a desperately thin donkey.

Tiredly, the young man asks, "Would you have a room?"

Without intending to, Jacob laughs. It is a cruel thing to do, but it is such a stupid question he cannot help himself. Regaining his composure, he says gruffly, "There's no room in the inn. Now be off with you."

"Wait. Wait," the young man pleads. "I am Joseph and this is Mary my wife. We have come a great distance and it's bitterly cold tonight."

And it is, true enough. Even as Jacob stands at the door, which is open just a crack, a gust of wind whips through the small opening, chilling him to the bone.

Seeing him shiver Joseph takes hope. "My wife is with child," he explains, "and her time is near."

Jacob hears her groan, or at least he thinks he does. *Still,* he reasons, *it could be the wind. Besides, it is no concern of mine.* Almost as an afterthought, he recommends a mid-wife and moves to close the door.

When he does Joseph leans against it, making it impossible for Jacob to close it. So they stand there — the determined young man and the innkeeper. Now Mary groans again.

There can be no mistaking it for the wind this time. Once more a bitterly cold gust of wind cuts the innkeeper to the bone.

"You must have something," Joseph says.

Desperately Jacob tries to think of something, anything, to rid himself of this persistent young man. Hannah joins him at the door, and hearing Joseph's plea she says, "They could share our room."

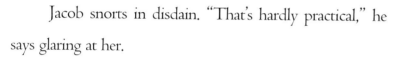

Jacob snorts in disdain. "That's hardly practical," he says glaring at her.

Now his mind is racing. *I must do something,* he thinks, *or Hannah will move them right into our room.*

Turning to the young couple, he says, "There's a sheep shed in back of the Inn. It's not much, I'll grant you, but it will shelter you from the cold. It's like a cave dug out of the side of the hill, with a small shed built over the opening to serve as a wind break."

Once more a soft groan escapes Mary's clamped lips, prompting Joseph to act. Turning to the innkeeper he says, "We'll take it." They haggle over the price briefly, but Joseph's heart isn't in it. Besides, he has no place else to go.

Wearily Jacob returns to his room, where he collapses on his bed, nearly overcome with exhaustion. But sleep won't come. Though Hannah has said nothing, he senses her displeasure. In the darkness, he defends himself against her unspoken disapproval. He is not insensitive, nor unkind. He did the best he could under the circumstances.

Flinging back the bedclothes, he throws a wrap around his shoulders and hunts his cushion. Glaring at Hannah, who pretends to be asleep, he demands, "You didn't really expect me to let them share our room, did you? That's hardly reasonable you know. They are total strangers. They seem honest enough, I'll grant you, but a man can never be too careful."

Hannah only grunts.

"I am not responsible," Jacob fumes in the darkness. "I had nothing to do with the predicament in which they find themselves. Is it my fault that she's pregnant? Is it my fault that Caesar Augustus ordered them to Bethlehem? Is it my fault there's no room in the inn? Indeed, if it hadn't been for my foresight, they wouldn't be the only weary travelers without a place to sleep on this cold night."

It's no use. Hannah will not exonerate him, nor will his conscience. Muttering under his breath, he tugs on his clothes. Hearing him thrashing about in the dark, Hannah lights a candle and looks at him questioningly. Gruffly he says, "I am going to take them some old blankets."

Getting out of bed, she makes her way to the fire and stirs it up. Reluctantly the coals come to life and in a matter of minutes she is heating soup.

When it is hot, Jacob lugs it, along with some thick bread and the blankets he has gathered, out to the sheep shed. Joseph receives these modest provisions gratefully, and the innkeeper returns to his quarters feeling almost noble. His conscience is clear. To his way of thinking, no one could do more.

By now it is quite late and he falls into an exhausted sleep. But he doesn't sleep well. He dreams the strangest dreams. Once it is something about angels, and then he dreams of the Messiah's birth, only it wasn't at all like he had been taught.

A little later he awakes to the sound of music. It is unlike anything he has ever heard— pure and clear, joyous beyond description. It seems to be coming from the hills overlooking Bethlehem, but how could that be, he wonders. Opening the shutters he gasps. "Hannah, come here. The sky is on fire."

Before she can rouse herself, the music fades and the fire disappears from the sky.

"Jacob, what is it?" she mumbles sleepily.

Ignoring her, Jacob closes the shutters and returns to bed. Sometime later he is awakened again. This time it is no dream, of that he is sure. The street below his window is filled with loud singing and rowdy laughter. In a fit of temper he hurls himself from the bed and tears the shutters open. Seeing a rather shabby band of shepherds, he curses them roundly.

"Be gone with you," he screams. "Give a hard working man a little rest."

Unfazed by his angry outburst they look at him with sheepish grins and go right on singing.

"What," he demands in his harshest voice, "do you have to sing about that can't wait until morning?"

In an instant they are all talking.

"We are celebrating the birth of the Messiah!" one of them announces, puffing himself up with self-importance.

Another says, "The whole sky broke open and there were angels everywhere. No one ever saw so many angels, not even our father Jacob at Bethel."

Attempting to humor them the innkeeper asks, "And where might this miraculous event have taken place?"

They look at each other in amazement and then one of them says, "Why it took place right here, in that sheep shed out behind your inn."

That is too much for Jacob! He slams the shutters closed and seeks the comfort of his bed.

It is business as usual the next day, and by the time Jacob thinks to check on the young man and his wife they are gone. For a few weeks the shepherds' wild story is the talk of Bethlehem, but no one really believes it. Jacob doesn't. After all, if there had been anything special about that young couple, he would have noticed it right off, wouldn't he?

CHAPTER SEVEN
The Birth

As he turns back toward the stable,

an unusually bright star catches his eye.

THE BIRTH

*I*t is dark when Joseph and Mary reach the stable, pitch black to be exact, and bitterly cold. Mary is nearly numb with exhaustion and stiff with cold as Joseph helps her dismount. Her feet and ankles are painfully swollen, making it difficult to walk. Leaning on Joseph's arm, she ducks into the stable. As she does she is seized with a sharp pain. Against her will she groans softly, causing Joseph's brow to furrow with concern. Hurriedly he arranges her bedding on a cushion of clean straw and gently helps her lie down.

For the hundredth time he wonders if he did the right thing in bringing her. Nazareth to Bethlehem is an easy enough journey for a man, but Mary is great with child, and five days on the road have totally exhausted her, leaving her looking pinched and haggard. Now she is about to give birth, and he doesn't know the first thing about midwifing, or where to find someone that does for that matter.

With an exaggerated deliberateness the old man extracts a small scroll from his bag and hands it to her.

After making her as comfortable as he can, Joseph tends to the donkey, leading it to the back of the cave, where several other beasts are feeding from troughs that have been chiseled in the virgin stone. Though he has had only limited experience with animals, he finds their presence comforting, the warmth of their body heat taking the edge off the chill of the night.

Moving back to the front of the cave, Joseph clears a space on the floor and builds a small a fire upon which he heats their meager provisions. Mary is too tired to eat and hardly touches her food, but he eats with an appetite. When they are finished, Mary huddles by the fire warming her hands, while he arranges a better pallet near the fire. Although it hardly diminishes the cold, it does give the illusion of comfort.

Soon Mary is asleep, or appears to be, and Joseph is lost in his thoughts. A gust of wind threatens the small fire and he hastily adds more wood, hoping he has enough to last the night. Once more he berates himself for getting Mary into such a mess. He had to come. Caesar Augustus' decree made that mandatory, but bringing Mary was his choice.

It was originally Mary's idea, to be sure, but the ultimate decision was his. There were a number of reasons he decided to bring her with him, not the least of which was her state of mind. The last few months had been trying beyond all imagining.

Although their parents were supportive, it was obvious enough that they gave little credence to their explanation regarding Mary's pregnancy. And, as might be expected, they were the subject of numerous rumors, none of them flattering — all of which made the thought of his absence unbearable for Mary, especially since the time of her delivery was near.

The thing that convinced him, though, happened in the synagogue two Sabbaths ago. As was customary there was a prayer, followed by a reading from the Torah and then one from the Prophets. Listening to the words of the ancient prophet Micah, his heart had leaped within him. "But you, Bethlehem Ephrathah, though you are small among the clans of Judah, out of you will come for me one who will be ruler over Israel, whose origins are from of old, from ancient times."

In that moment he realized that it had been prophesied that the Messiah would be born in Bethlehem. With that understanding his perspective changed. No longer was Caesar's decree just a monumental inconvenience; rather, it was part of God's eternal plan. Nor was Mary's desire to go to Bethlehem just the irrational whim of an emotionally distraught mother-to-be. No, it was the inner prompting of God's Holy Spirit.

In the comfort and safety of Nazareth it all seemed so clear, so logical, and he had hastened to trade some woodwork for a small donkey upon which Mary could ride. Now he cannot help but question his judgment. If coming to Bethlehem was really part of God's plan, then why was the trip so hard on Mary? Why did God not spare her the pain and discomfort that have left her completely exhausted? And why was there no place for them in the inn?

Drawing his cloak close about him, Joseph huddles nearer the fire. The wind seems to be rising and it is going to be a long night, of that he is sure. Mary groans, shivering from the cold. Reluctantly, Joseph removes his cloak and places it over her, for there is nothing else. Already she is ensconced in his bedroll as well as her own. Turning back to the fire, he stretches his hands toward its meager warmth.

From the darkness a voice calls, "Hello!"

Before Joseph can answer, the innkeeper ducks into the cave bearing an armload of things. "I've brought you some blankets," he says brusquely. "And the wife made you some hot soup."

Without waiting for Joseph to respond, he deposits the provisions near the fire and turns to go. Belatedly Joseph attempts to thank him, but already he has disappeared into the night — anxious, no doubt, to return to his comfortable quarters. And who could blame him?

After heating the soup Joseph moves to Mary's side. She is awake and he helps her sit up so she can eat. The soup is hot and thick, and as she eats a little color returns to her cheeks.

Suddenly she gasps with pain. It only lasts a moment and when it passes he asks, "Are you all right?"

"I think so," she says, in voice grown small with fear.

She has no more interest in food, so he tucks the blankets around her before returning to the fire, where he heats the rest of the soup for himself. Finding the bread and soup to his liking he quickly devours it, using a crust of bread to wipe the bowl clean.

Filled and slightly warmed, Joseph dozes by the fire, awaking from time to time to add a handful of sticks. Ever so often he hears Mary gasp with pain, but he is simply too tired to comprehend what is happening.

Sometime in the wee hours of the morning Mary calls out, her voice reaching him through the befogging maze of an exhausted sleep. "Joseph," she groans, "please help me."

With an effort he rouses himself and goes to her side. Though the cold is numbing, her hair is damp with sweat and tiny beads of perspiration glisten on her lip. As he kneels beside her, she is seized by another contraction and bites her lip to keep from crying out.

When it passes she lies back, gasping for breath. That she is in labor is apparent even to his inexperienced eye. It is not unexpected — the first pains started late in the afternoon — still he feels overwhelmed. He doesn't know what to do. He is afraid to leave Mary by herself, yet he must find a midwife. Perhaps the innkeeper's wife will stay with her while he goes in search of one.

Another contraction seizes Mary, and in spite of her determination not to cry out, she wails in pain. By now her contractions are coming fast and hard, with hardly a break between them. There is no time to waste. He must find a midwife and fast. Frantically, he lunges to his feet and starts into the night.

"Joseph!" she screams, stopping him in his tracks. "Joseph, help me. The baby is coming."

Returning to where she lies panting on the cold ground, he kneels beside her feeling absolutely helpless. He has never seen anything born. He is a carpenter, not a shepherd or a farmer. What does he know about giving birth?

Between gasps she says, "Joseph, you must catch the baby. Don't let him touch the cold ground."

Now things are happening fast, leaving him dazed and uncertain. Though Mary is in the travail of labor, she directs his every action. With one final push, she delivers a son into his huge, work-hardened hands.

"Cut the cord," she instructs him, "and tie it."

Clumsily he does as he is told, marveling all the time at the miracle of birth. He cannot help thinking that this tiny creature, so ordinary looking, is none other than the only begotten Son of God. *Though it is nearly inconceivable,* he thinks, *God has become one of us.*

"Joseph!" Mary's voice jerks him from his musing. "Clean him up and give him to me before he catches a death of cold."

There is no water to bath the baby, who is now squalling his protest at being thrust from the warmth of his mother's womb into the cold of the stable. Taking some pieces of clean cloth which Mary has prepared for this very purpose, Joseph rubs him clean, marveling at the perfection of his tiny fingers and toes.

Though she is completely worn out, Mary reaches for her son. "Jesus," she whispers, as Joseph gently places him in her arms. Hugging him to her breast, she says, "My son and my Lord."

Staring at them in wonder, Joseph hears again the words of the angel: "What is conceived in her is from the Holy Spirit. She will give birth to a son, and you are to give him the name Jesus, because he will save his people from their sins."

Now that the excitement is over, he finds that he is trembling with wonder. Staring at his hands he thinks, *These callused carpenter's hands helped bring the Son of God into the world, and that tiny baby, nursing now at his mother's breast, is God incarnate.*

Mary flashes him a smile. He thinks his heart will break, so great is his love for her. Shyly she asks, "Joseph, did you ever think that the Son of God would sleep in my arms?"

He wants to say something, anything, but words fail him. Instead he kneels beside her and watches as she wraps baby Jesus in strips of cloth, then lays him in the manger, where she has prepared him a bed.

At last the stable grows quiet, and in the distance he hears faintly the sound of music. Moving outside in order to hear more clearly, he cannot help but notice that the sky is unusually bright above the hills surrounding Bethlehem. From a distance there comes the faint sound of singing. Though he cannot make out the words, even to his untrained ear the harmony is extraordinary. For a moment he is transfixed, so pure and holy is it. Then it is gone, and with it the light. Once more the sky is just a wide expanse of starlight.

As he turns back toward the stable, an unusually bright star catches his eye. As unlikely as it seems, it appears to be positioned directly over the place where baby Jesus lies in the manger. It seems nearer, somehow, than all the others — and brighter. How appropriate, Joseph thinks, for the prophets refer to Jesus as the bright morning star.

Jesus is asleep when Joseph reenters the stable. As he breathes, his breath is clearly visible in the cold. Hastily Joseph turns his attention to the fire, which has now burned down to a handful of stubborn coals. Carefully he adds fuel, a few sticks at a time, until it is burning brightly once more.

In its flickering light he watches Mary as she keeps her vigil beside the manger. Though she is weary beyond words, she seems to have found an inner strength that now sustains her. How blessed he is to have such a woman as his wife.

Leaving the fire, he kneels beside her and slips his arm around her waist. For a few minutes neither of them speaks. Then Mary says, "Thank you Joseph. Your love these past months have been my strength. I don't know how I could have done it without you."

Resting her head against his shoulder, she falls into an exhausted sleep while he contemplates the future. In the morning he must find a place for them to live. They simply cannot spend another night in this dung-infested sheep shed. And if they are to remain in Bethlehem, he will have to find work. Surely there must be a carpenter who can use a skilled woodworker.

Being a responsible husband and father, Joseph is concerned about such things, but he is not worried. God will provide, of that he is sure. Jesus is His son, and God will not allow anything to happen to him. By now Joseph's own eyes are heavy with sleep and he allows himself to doze off, secure in the knowledge of God's provision.

CHAPTER EIGHT
The Shepherds

Suddenly the stillness of the night is

broken by a baby's whimper

THE SHEPHERDS

*I*t is still dark when Joseph awakes, and for a moment he is not sure what woke him. Jesus is sleeping peacefully and so is Mary, her breathing deep and regular. Once more the fire is down to a few stubborn embers, but he cannot bring himself to brave the cold in order to feed it. He is nearing sleep again when he hears a movement in the dark, just outside the stable, then voices. He cannot make out what they are saying, but from the sound of it there must be several men, at least four or five.

Mary puts her hand on his arm, her eyes wide with fright. Motioning for her to be still, Joseph slips toward the small opening that serves as the entrance. As he does, he quickly scans the stable's dark interior, searching for anything that might serve as a weapon. Earlier he had noticed a piece of a shepherd's staff among a pile of rubbish, and now he lays hold of it, taking some comfort in its stoutness.

Squatting in the deep shadows just inside the stable, he sees several men silhouetted against the pre-dawn sky. They appear rough and unkempt, and he doesn't relish a confrontation. Hopefully they will move on without discovering the cave.

"An angel of the Lord appeared to me, to all of us that is."

They are arguing heatedly now, and their words carry clearly to Joseph's ears.

"I don't care what you think you remember," a weary voice declares, "I say we come back in the morning when we can see."

"How can you even think such a thing?" a small man demands impatiently. "This is the chance of a lifetime and you want to wait until morning. You've got to be out of your mind!"

"Continue the search if you want," the first man says, "but I've had enough for one night."

With that he turns on his heel and heads down the hill. After a moment the others turn to follow him, all but the small man who is shaking his head in disgust. Inside the stable Joseph breathes a sign of relief.

Suddenly the stillness of the night is broken by a baby's whimper. Although it is hardly more than a whisper, there is no mistaking the sound. Mary moves quickly to hush baby Jesus, but it is no use. Now the whimper turns into a full-fledged wail, carrying clearly to the departing men. Turning, they retrace their steps up the hill. There is nothing for Joseph to do except confront them. Taking a firm grip on the broken shepherd's staff, he steps into the night.

"What can I do for you men?" he asks, trying to keep his voice from shaking.

With more than a hint of triumph, the lone man turns to his companions and says, "I told you they had to be here."

The others fall in behind him as he hurries toward Joseph. Excitedly, he says, "We have come to see the Savior, Christ the Lord, who was born this night in Bethlehem the town of David."

Without waiting for a reply, he pushes past Joseph and into the small stable, where Mary is trying to quiet baby Jesus. At the sight of the child, a holy hush falls over him. He kneels awkwardly before the manger, staring in wonder at the mother and her baby.

Joseph moves to Mary's side and slips his arm around her shoulders protectively, while the others crowd into the cramped space before the manger. Finally Mary asks, "How did you learn about Jesus?"

Nervously, they glance at each other. They are obviously uncomfortable, and well they should be, for they are shepherds. There was a time when keeping sheep was an honorable profession in Israel, but that time is long past. Now they are a despised lot, known for their deceitfulness and ceremonial uncleanness. Not only is their testimony not accepted in the formal proceedings of Jewish courts, but they are also prohibited from entering the synagogue on the Sabbath.

Finally, the little man who first spoke to Joseph takes it upon himself to speak for the group. "I'm a shepherd," he says, "as are my friends. Earlier tonight a most extraordinary thing happened to us. Our flocks were in the fold for the night and we were sitting around our fire swapping stories, like we do most every night.

"After awhile I went to check on the sheep. On my way back I stopped on an outcropping of rock to study the sky. The night was beautiful, clear, with stars as big as lanterns. Close too. It seemed I could reach out and touch them. It was cold though, real cold, with a biting wind that cut to the bone.

"I don't know how to tell you what happened next," he says, staring at the stable floor uncomfortably. "You probably won't believe me, but what I am going to tell you is the absolute truth. With God as my judge, I do not lie."

His companions look at each other and nod their heads solemnly. Taking courage from them, he continues. "An angel of the Lord appeared to me, to all of us that is."

Pausing again, he looks directly at Joseph. "You do believe in angels don't you?"

"Of course we do," says Joseph, encouraging him to get on with his story.

"You probably think it's exciting to see an angel, but you're wrong," he says. "There isn't anything exciting about it. It's terrifying. That's what it is, terrifying! If you ever find yourself face-to-face with an angel you'll know what I mean. With the glory of the Lord shining all around you there's only one thing you can think about."

Pausing, he waits until Joseph asks, "And what might that be?"

"Your sins!" he says, "Your sins. At least that's the way it was for me. I thought of every rotten thing I ever did. How vain the littleness of my life seemed in the light of his presence, how petty my concerns. Surely, I thought, this is the end of the world. The judgment of God has come and I have been found out, caught red-handed. And you know what the angel said to me?"

"'Don't be afraid,' the angel said. Can you believe that? Don't be afraid! Well, if you had any sense at all, you'd be afraid. I had good sense, and I was terrified. You would be too."

He didn't have to convince either Mary or Joseph. They knew all about angelic encounters, and they knew about fear.

"Then the angel told me the most amazing thing. He said, 'Today in the town of David a Savior has been born to you; he is Christ the Lord. This will be a sign to you: You will find a baby wrapped in cloths and lying in a manger.'

"Suddenly the whole sky was full of angels singing and praising God. They lit up the night so you couldn't tell if it was daylight or dark. And such singing it was, the likes of which I've never heard. Songs so sweet and pure I thought surely I had died and gone to Abraham's bosom.

"Then it was over. Right before my eyes the angels began to ascend into heaven. Slowly they faded from sight, taking their song with them, but leaving my heart strangely warmed.

"The whole thing didn't last long — hardly as long as it takes me to tell about it — and then they were gone. Once more the sky was empty except for the distant stars, the night was quiet, except for the bleating of the sheep and the moan of the wind.

"Hurrying back to camp I found my companions rubbing their eyes and looking at each other. 'What's going on?' I asked, but they answered me not a word. Not that I blame them. When you are in the midst of an experience like that you know it's real. But when it's over, and things are back to normal, you wonder if it really happened.

"Now it's just ordinary things again — sheep dung and mud on your sandals, cold wind cutting through your cloak — you know, things like that. Then you wonder. Then you ask yourself, did it really happen or did I imagine it?

"Finally one of the guys asked: 'Did you see anything?'

"'Like what?' I demanded.

"Then everyone began talking at once, only no one would come right out and say what they saw. Finally, I took the plunge: 'There must have been a million angels,' I said. 'The whole sky was full of them. They were all singing and praising God.'

"That was all it took. Once I said that, everyone begin talking at once.

"'Let's go to Bethlehem,' someone suggested, 'and see this thing that has happened, which the Lord has told us about.'

"'What about the sheep?'

"'The sheep are in the field. They will be all right.'

"Then we were off to Bethlehem. With no thought for our safety, we went running through the dark, tripping and sliding down one muddy hillside after another. We were driven, every one of us, to know if this incredible thing that the angels had told us was true."

By now his face is animated, and he gestures wildly as he talks. His fellow shepherds are nodding and laughing.

"You should have seen us," he says. "It was late when we got to Bethlehem, well past midnight, and the town was closed up tight. But we knew where to look. The angel told us He would be lying in a manger, so we started checking out barns.

"In and out of barns we ran, doors slamming in the wind, laughing and crying in our joy.

"'Is he here?'

"'No. Nothing but animals in here.'

"After awhile our enthusiasm began to wear thin. We were tired and cold. We had searched every stable and sheep shed in all of Bethlehem without finding a trace of a baby.

"We were about to give up when I remembered this place. It's hardly a barn — just a cave really — with a make-shift shelter across the front, and nearly impossible to find in the dark...."

His voice trails off and he looks around the stable, as if seeing it for the first time. It was never more than a crude shelter at best, and years of disservice hadn't improved it. The smells linger — animal smells, urine-damp straw, and sheep dung. But that isn't what he sees. In his eyes this hole in the wall is a holy place.

He looks at Mary with a reverence Joseph has seldom seen. And seeing her through his eyes is, for Joseph, like seeing her for the very first time. She's just a child, a girl really, not yet fourteen, and of a peasant family. Yet, in another sense she belongs to the ages. The favor of God has set her apart, made her unique among women.

Now the shepherd looks at Joseph, who grows uncomfortable beneath his stare. He cannot help but wonder how he appears in the shepherd's eyes. He is an ordinary man, a little taller than most, but nondescript in every other way. His hands are large, even for a man of his height, and callused from years of work in the carpenter shop. No doubt the shepherd must be wondering why God should choose a man like him — a thought that has crossed Joseph's mind more than once.

But all of that is secondary. The shepherds have not come to see Mary nor Joseph. Now they have eyes only for the baby lying in the manger. It is obvious that they want to touch him, but they don't know if they dare. The little shepherd's face says it all. Though Jesus looks like any other baby, he knows, as sure as he has ever known anything, that this baby is God. Yahweh in a manger!

He and the other shepherds stare transfixed for ever so long as they kneel in the dirty straw before the manger. Then they humbly bow their heads in worship. For a moment Joseph is shocked. It goes against everything he has been taught from childhood, but Mary is unfazed. She doesn't seem at all surprised that they would kneel and worship him.

Not wanting to tire Mary or the child, the shepherds back out of the stable, hardly speaking, so real is the sense of the Lord's nearness. Once outside, however, they break loose — hugging one another and pounding each other on the back, laughing and talking, praising God in loud voices.

Returning to Mary and the baby, Joseph finds her deep in thought. Once more he stirs up the fire and sets about preparing breakfast. As he works, his thoughts turn to the shepherds. He cannot help wondering how this experience will change their lives. In a lot of ways things will be the same — same cold wind and damp ground, same sheep and poverty — but in another way nothing will ever be the same again, for no man can look God in the face without being changed.

In time the memory of the angels will fade, as will their recollection of Mary and Joseph, but forever they will remember the baby Jesus — God wrapped in swaddling clothes, lying in a manger.

CHAPTER NINE

Simeon

He is about to give up when,

at last, he spots a young couple purchasing

two pigeons.

SIMEON

Awaking early, Simeon makes his way to the temple court for morning prayer, as he has done all of his adult life. Though he sees a number of familiar faces, there is no one whom he could really call a friend. Most of his contemporaries have gone the way of all flesh, and the few who remain no longer dwell in Jerusalem.

While waiting for the call to prayer his mind turns to the past, as it often does these days. For years he served as a scribe, translating the Holy Scriptures from the Hebrew language into the Greek language. As both a scholar and a devout man, he took great pleasure in his work; that is, until it fell his lot to translate the prophet Isaiah.

Well does he remember his confusion upon first reading, "The Lord himself will give you a sign: The virgin will be with child and will give birth to a son, and will call him Immanuel." He threw down his pen in outrage. What kind of a verse was this? Had the prophet lost his mind? Virgins do not bear children! Neither does God stoop to become a man!

Holding that holy child, Simeon experiences a sense of completeness unlike anything he has ever known in his long life.

Refusing to translate the text, he returned to his home in a huff. That very night the Lord came to him and spoke to his spirit. He made him know that he would not die until he saw that prophecy fulfilled with his own eyes!

Initially he doubted the Lord's message, but as the years passed so did his doubts. He has now outlived nearly all of his contemporaries. As far as he can determine, the only reason he is still alive is because he has not yet laid eyes on the virgin's son, the Lord's Christ, the one Isaiah said will be called Immanuel.

The call to prayer now echoes over the temple courts, returning his thoughts to the present. Though his joints are stiff with age, he kneels on the hard pavers and presses his forehead low to the ground. While reciting the familiar Psalms, his heart cries out to God. "Is this the day, O, Lord," he prays, "when these tired eyes shall finally see the consolation of Israel?"

Unlike other days, he now senses a stirring deep in his spirit. At first it is nothing more than a hint of a feeling, the faintest of impressions, but as he waits before the Lord it becomes more distinct. By the time he leaves the place of prayer, he is absolutely convinced that this is the day.

Moved by the Spirit, he wanders the temple courts awaiting a sign. Although he has no idea what kind of sign to expect, he is confident that he will recognize it when it comes.

Since it is not Passover week, the temple courts are busy, but not thronged. Here and there itinerant rabbis hold court, expounding the Scriptures. Occasionally the piercing wail of a newly circumcised son can be heard above the murmur of conversation, as can the transactions of the money changers and those who sell birds and animals for sacrifice.

By now it is nearly mid-morning. Simeon's old bones are growing weary, when he senses a rising excitement in his spirit. Anxiously he scans the crowd, searching for a sign. Nothing. He is about to give up when, at last, he spots a young couple purchasing two pigeons. That they are poor is obvious, for only the most destitute cannot afford a lamb for sacrifice, yet he senses a richness in their spirit.

There is something especially touching about the way they look at each other, as if they share a secret the world cannot know. From time to time she peeks at a baby, wrapped in blankets and cradled against her breast. When she does her face seems to glow. Just watching her makes Simeon's heart ache.

Working his way through the crowd as fast as his arthritic knees will take him, he stops directly in front of the young woman and extends his gnarled hands to receive her baby. His sudden appearance startles her, and for a moment fear fills her eyes. And well it might, for Simeon is stooped and toothless, with knotty hands.

Her husband steps up beside her and puts his arm around her waist. When he does the fear leaves her face and she smiles uncertainly as she places her baby in the old priest's hands. Holding that holy child, Simeon experiences a sense of completeness unlike anything he has ever known in his long life.

Intuitively he knows that in his hands he holds the fulfillment of Isaiah's prophecy. Although this infant looks for all the world like any other baby, he is different. His mother is a virgin and God Himself is his father.

Suddenly the Spirit of the Lord comes upon Simeon and he begins to prophesy: "Sovereign Lord, as you have promised, you now dismiss your servant in peace. For my eyes have seen your salvation, which you have prepared in the sight of all people, a light for revelation to the Gentiles and for glory to your people Israel."

For a moment Simeon can hardly believe what he has said. Salvation and a light of revelation to the Gentiles? What kind of prophecy can this be? The Messiah is Israel's deliverer, the one who will triumph over her enemies.

Intellectually he can make no sense of these strange ideas, yet his soul is soaring. He should feel betrayed, but he doesn't. Instead of resenting the idea that this child is the Savior of all nations, rather than of Israel alone, he feels exhilarated. In this moment God has enlarged his spirit, and delivered him from his provincialism.

A crowd of curious onlookers press close about them, and others are coming from the temple courts. Making her way through them is Anna the prophetess. She is well-known to those who serve in the temple, having lived here nearly all of her life. Since her husband died more than sixty years ago, she has never left this sacred place. Night and day she gives herself to worship, fasting and praying continually.

Taking the baby from Simeon, she lifts him toward the Lord and gives thanks in a loud voice. "Sovereign Lord," she prays, "great is your mercy and grace toward Your people. You have manifested Your love for us in that while we were still sinners You have sent Your Son to live among us and to deliver us from our sins."

Turning to the crowd she proclaims: "This is no ordinary baby. He is the promised one, the deliverer of Israel. Of the increase of his government and peace there will be no end. He will reign on David's throne and over his kingdom, establishing and upholding it with justice and righteousness from that time on and forever.

"The Spirit of the Lord will rest on him — the Spirit of wisdom and of understanding, the Spirit of counsel and of power, the Spirit of knowledge and of the fear of the Lord.

"He is the prophet of whom Moses spoke saying, 'The Lord your God will raise up for you a prophet like me from among your own brothers. You must listen to him.'"

Returning the baby to his mother, she enfolds both mother and child in her bony arms. What a sight they make — a wrinkled old prophetess and a fresh faced virgin mother. Together they worship the child and God the Father who gave him.

Once more the Spirit of the Lord comes upon Simeon. Stepping forward, he places his hand upon the child's tiny head. "This child," he prophecies, "is destined to cause the falling and rising of many in Israel, and to be a sign that will be spoken against, so that the thoughts of many hearts will be revealed."

Looking the virgin mother full in the face, he continues in a voice that is now heavy with sorrow. "And a sword will pierce your own soul too."

In an instant Mary's joyous tears are dried up, leaving dirty smudges on her cheeks. Confusion and fear flood her face. Desperately she turns to her husband, searching his face for some explanation. Finding none, she turns back to Simeon, clutching his arm with her free hand.

"What do you mean," she demands in a voice made ragged with fear, "a sword will pierce my soul too?"

She places special emphasis on the word "too," and he knows she is thinking of her son and not of herself. Already she loves him more than she could ever love herself.

Gladly would she lay down her life to spare his.

Though he is tempted to speak words of comfort, to try in some way to temper the fearful prophecy he has given, he says nothing. Integrity will not permit it. Instead he places his hands upon the heads of both the man and his wife and says: "The Lord bless you and keep you; the Lord make his face shine upon you and be gracious to you; the Lord turn his face toward you and give you peace."

Silently they take their leave. Simeon watches as they make their way toward the priest, where they will consecrate their son unto the Lord. Later they will sacrifice the two pigeons, one for a burnt offering and the other for a sin offering, in keeping with the Law of Moses.

Though he empathizes with the virgin mother, he cannot deny his joy. At long last the supreme purpose of his life has been realized. With his own eyes he has seen the salvation of the Lord. He has held God incarnate in his own hands!

He is now ready to die, and thus he prays, "Lord, now let your servant depart in peace, according to your word. For my eyes have seen your salvation."

CHAPTER TEN
The Escape

Without speaking,
they quickly remove boxes of various sizes from the bundler
on the camels and turn toward the house.

THE ESCAPE

Returning from Jerusalem, following the consecration of Jesus, Mary and Joseph settle into their new life in Bethlehem. In many ways it is a welcome reprieve from Nazareth with its rumors and innuendoes. Although they dearly miss their families, it is a relief to be free from the whispers that have plagued their hasty marriage from the beginning. In Bethlehem no one stares at them or questions the legitimacy of Jesus' birth.

Being good with his hands, Joseph soon builds a small but solid business. Of him it is said, "If you want something done right, take it to Joseph the carpenter." In the evenings he often whittles toys from pieces of scrap wood for his firstborn son.

Though she is hardly more than a girl herself, Mary is a devoted wife and mother, filling the tiny room they call home with love and laughter. Never does Joseph tire of watching her as she goes about her womanly duties. Not infrequently he stops his whittling to gaze at her as she nurses Jesus and prepares him for bed.

"We have brought gifts for the one who has been born King of the Jews."

The only blot on their happiness is the haunting memory of Simeon's fateful words. Though Mary has tried to thrust them from her mind, they refuse to budge. Like an everlasting echo she hears them again and again: "...and a sword will pierce your own soul too."

Try as she might, she can make no sense of them, nor can she escape the fearful premonition they have birthed in her. Of one thing she is certain — the prophecy has something to do with her son. He is in danger, of that she is sure.

The nights are the worst. Sleep will not come, and when it does, she is tormented with terrifying dreams in which baby Jesus is torn from her arms and put to death. More than once she has awakened screaming, bathed in a cold sweat, the taste of fear bitter in her mouth. Joseph does what he can, but Mary will not be comforted, not as long as she feels Jesus is in danger.

————)((O)) ————

In Jerusalem, King Herod is nearing the end of his bloody reign. An impostor to the throne, an Idumean, he is ever suspicious. In the course of his reign he has murdered friend and foe alike, anyone whom he imagines might be a threat to his crown. Among the victims of his paranoia are several members of his own family, including three sons and his second wife, Mariamne, a Hasmonean woman of pure Jewish blood whose family had produced priests and rulers in Judea for the past one hundred years.

Now his health is failing and he is in constant pain. He can no longer walk without help, and even then the pain is nearly more than he can bear. His joints are stiff and badly swollen, especially his lower legs and feet, which are turning black from lack of circulation. Not surprisingly, his legendary cruelty and paranoia increase in direct proportion to his failing health.

It is little wonder then that the arrival of an unannounced envoy from the East should arouse his suspicions, especially when it is reported they are seeking one who has just been born King of the Jews. News of their mission sweeps the Holy City, creating a great excitement. There is talk of little else. Everywhere people congregate there is speculation about the Messiah's birth.

In the palace Herod is nearly beside himself. If indeed the son of David has been born, the so-called Anointed One, then he must be found and put to death. He must not be allowed to live and reclaim the throne of his father David.

Calling for the chief priests and teachers of the law, Herod inquires of them where the Messiah is to be born. Taking the scroll of the prophet Micah, a priest reads it aloud in the king's hearing: "But you, Bethlehem, in the land of Judah, are by no means least among the rulers of Judah; for out of you will come a ruler who will be the shepherd of my people Israel."

Having learned what he sought, the old king now dismisses the religious leaders with a curt wave of his hand. Already his cunning mind is seeking a way to utilize this new information to his advantage. In short order he considers and discards a half a dozen schemes before settling on one to his liking. Smiling grimly, he calls for his secretary and issues a series of orders before falling into an exhausted sleep.

Early the next day the Magi present themselves at the palace as the king's summons directed. Entering his private apartment, they discover not the royal dignitary they anticipated, but an emaciated old man nearly immobilized by pain. Disguising their shock, they pay him homage, bowing deeply.

Feigning piety, Herod addresses these wise men from the East in an oily voice. "I am told that you have information regarding the birth of our long awaited Messiah."

"Yes, your majesty. We saw his star when it rose and we have come to worship him."

"Where might he be found?" asks the King, contriving a smile. "Tell me, that I too may go and worship him."

After a painful silence, one of the Magi respond. "We have not been able to locate him. He is nowhere to be found in Jerusalem."

"Ah, then perhaps I may be of service to you. One of our prophets has written that he will be born in Bethlehem, the city of David. Perhaps you will find him there."

"Thank you, sire."

"Bethlehem is but a short journey south of here. Go and make a careful search for the child. As soon as you find him report to me, so that I too may go and worship him."

Watching them depart, Herod smiles grimly. It was easier than he expected. Foreigners are so naive, so easily taken in. Soon he will put an end to this "King of the Jews."

<hr>

Entering Bethlehem astride their camels, the Magi immediately attract a crowd. At first it is only children, but soon they are joined by adults, both men and women. The dignity and mystery surrounding the three foreigners is irresistible to the common folk, for whom excitement is in short supply.

The contrast between the shabbiness of Bethlehem and the pomp and ceremony that accompanies the wise men is readily apparent, but the Magi pay it no mind. Their eyes are fixed steadfastly on the star that first appeared to them in the East. As afternoon turns into evening, it blazes ever more brightly and now situates itself directly over a nondescript house on the far edge of the village.

Halting in front of the house, the foreigners dismount and beat the dust from their brightly colored robes. If they are shocked by the poverty into which the infant king has been born, they do not show it. Without speaking, they quickly remove boxes of various sizes from the bundles on the camels and turn toward the house. Drawing near they pause for a moment, their faces flushed with excitement. Finally the tallest one steps forward and raises his hand to rap on the door.

Inside the tiny house Mary bends over a small fire, preparing the evening meal. Jesus plays in the far corner, the toys carved by Joseph scattered about him. It has been nearly two years since she gave birth, still hardly a day goes by but what she relives it all in her mind. Now, as at other times, she remembers the wonder of his birth and the shepherds who came to worship him.

Suddenly her reminiscing is interrupted by a loud banging on the door. As always, her first thought is of Jesus. She scoops him up as she makes her way toward the front of the house. Peeking through a crack she sees three men, foreigners by the looks of them. Behind them, kneeling in the street, she catches sight of their camels.

When she opens the door, they stare at her without speaking, but more especially at the child in her arms. Slowly, at first just one of them, then all three kneel in the dirt before the door, bowing their heads. Fascinated by the bright colors of their robes and their tall pointed hats, Jesus waves his arms and laughs, reaching for the nearest one.

With their faces pressed to the ground, they pay homage to the infant king. Finally one of them speaks. "We have brought gifts for the one who has been born King of the Jews."

"Please come in," Mary says, regaining her composure.

Where is Joseph, she wonders, wishing he was here with her. *He would know what to do.*

Once they are inside the house she turns to face her guests, experiencing a momentary twinge of embarrassment when she realizes the tiny room can hardly accommodate all of them. Before she can speak they kneel once more, leaning forward until their foreheads are pressed against the floor. Still kneeling, they each in turn place a box at Mary's feet.

Opening his box, the first man displays a heavy gold chain upon which is fastened a shiny medallion of the same substance. It is obviously expensive, beyond anything Mary can imagine, and she gasps. The man simply smiles and bows his head once more.

From his box the second man removes cakes of frankincense, very costly. "A gift," he says, "for the King of the Jews."

The third man holds up a small flask, delicately made and beautiful. "Oil of myrrh," he whispers, carefully sitting it at Mary's feet.

By now her mind is racing, her thoughts a mixture of wonder and fear. If King Herod learns of this he will not rest until he has killed Jesus, of this she is sure. To his Jewish subjects he is known as "that murderous old man," and not without cause. On another level, though, she marvels at the grace of God. Surely she is the mother of the Anointed One, the King of kings, before whom every knee shall bow.

With heads bowed the Magi back out of the room, leaving Mary holding Jesus in her arms, still in awe of everything that has transpired. At last she moves to the door and watches as they mount their camels and disappear into the gathering dusk.

The pain has returned with a vengeance, causing the old king to writhe in agony. Yet it is nothing compared with the torment in his mind. For three days he has awaited the return of the wise men, only to learn that they have deceived him. Having played them for fools, he realizes too late that it is he who has been made the fool. Rather than return to Jerusalem as they had agreed, the Magi, being warned by God in a dream, have escaped to their own country.

Though it is the dead of night, Herod rings for his secretary, who arrives bleary-eyed. Upon entering the king's private chamber, he immediately notes a new level of madness. Pain and paranoia have pushed the old monarch over the edge, and he now rages with homicidal fury.

It will be a dangerous night, the secretary notes, determining to watch his every word. One false step and his life will be finished, no matter that he has served Herod faithfully all these years.

Impatiently Herod demands, "What do you know of this one who is born King of the Jews."

"There is only one King of the Jews," he answers, choosing his words carefully, "and he is Herod the Great. Anyone who claims otherwise is a traitor."

"Enough," the old king hisses impatiently. "Enough! This is not about your loyalty. If it were, you would already be dead."

Bowing slightly, the secretary waits for him to continue.

"There is a conspiracy afoot, of that you can be sure. But it will not succeed. I will destroy this one who is called the king of the Jews, as I have destroyed all the others who aspired to my throne."

A wild light dances in his rheumy eyes as his crackling laughter echoes in the wide room. "Not only will I destroy this so-called child king," he wheezes noisily, "but I will strike fear into the heart of anyone who would dare covet my throne."

"What do you have in mind, my Lord?"

"In due time," the old king growls. "In due time."

Though Herod issues a decree designed to eliminate this child born King of the Jews, he fails. On the same night that the Magi departed, an angel of the Lord appeared to Joseph in a dream. "Get up," he said, "take the child and his mother and escape to Egypt. Stay there until I tell you, for Herod is going to search for the child to kill him."

Only after Herod is dead do Mary and Joseph feel it is safe to return to their own country. Even then, they do not dare return to Bethlehem, for fear that Herod's son Archelaus, who now reigns in Judea in his father's stead, might make another attempt on Jesus' life. Instead they return to Nazareth, in the district of Galilee. There Jesus grows in wisdom and stature, and in favor with God and men.

Epilogue

All the armies that ever marched, and all the governments that ever sat,

and all the kings that ever reigned, have not effected life upon this earth as powerfully

as has that One Solitary Life.

ONE SOLITARY LIFE

He was born in an obscure village, the child of a peasant woman. He worked in a carpentry shop until he was thirty, and then for three years he was an itinerant preacher.

When the tide of popular opinion turned against him, his friends ran away. He was turned over to his enemies. He was tried and convicted. He was nailed upon a cross between two thieves. When he was dead, he was laid in a borrowed grave.

He never wrote a book. He never held an office. He never owned a home. He never went to college. He never traveled more than two hundred miles from the place where he was born. He never did one of the things that usually accompanies greatness.

Yet all the armies that ever marched, and all the governments that ever sat, and all the kings that ever reigned, have not effected life upon this earth as powerfully as has that One Solitary Life.

- AUTHOR UNKNOWN

ENDNOTES

CHAPTER ONE

The story of Zechariah is based upon the Gospel of Luke, chapter one, in the *Holy Bible*. See also Malachi 3:1; 4:5,6 and Numbers 6:24-26. For more information, I suggest "The Gospel of Luke," p. 62, from *The New International Commentary On The New Testament*, by Norval Geldenhuys.

CHAPTER TWO

The story of Mary is based upon the Gospel of Luke, chapter one, in the *Holy Bible*. See also Deuteronomy 22:13-27, especially verses 23 and 24.

CHAPTER THREE

The story of Elizabeth is based upon the Gospel of Luke, chapter one, in the *Holy Bible*. See also Genesis 17:15-21; 21:1-7; 25:21; 30:1,22,23; and 1 Samuel 1:1-20.

CHAPTER FOUR

The story of Mary's return to Nazareth is based upon the Gospel of Luke, chapter one, and Matthew, chapter 1, in the *Holy Bible*. See also Isaiah 7:14.

CHAPTER FIVE

The story of Joseph is based upon the Gospel of Matthew, chapter one, in the *Holy Bible*. See also Psalm 118:24; Deuteronomy 22:23,24; and Isaiah 7:14. For more

information, I suggest "Matthew," from *The Communicator's Commentary*, by Myron S. Augsburger.

CHAPTER SIX

The story of the Innkeeper is based upon the Gospel of Luke, chapter 2, in the *Holy Bible*. See also Genesis 28:10-17.

CHAPTER SEVEN

The story of the birth of Jesus is based upon the Gospel of Luke, chapters one and two, in the *Holy Bible*. See also Matthew 1:20,21; Micah 5:2; and Numbers 24:17.

CHAPTER EIGHT

The story of the shepherds is based upon the Gospel of Luke, chapter two, in the *Holy Bible*. For more information, I suggest *What Child Is This?* by Rubel Shelly.

CHAPTER NINE

The story of Simeon is based upon the Gospel of Luke, chapter two, in the *Holy Bible*. See also Isaiah 7:14; 9:7; 11:12; and Numbers 6:24-26.

CHAPTER TEN

The story of Mary, Joseph, and Jesus' escape from Herod is based upon the Gospel of Matthew, chapter two in the *Holy Bible*. See also Luke 2:35.

ABOUT THE AUTHOR

Richard Exley is a man with a rich diversity of ministerial experience — pastor, author, radio host, and conference and retreat speaker. Serving as the senior pastor of Christian Chapel in Tulsa, Oklahoma, for many years, he was able to combine sensitive insights and a masterful use of language to speak candidly of the things most of us feel, but have never been able to put into words.

Exley is a gifted communicator, as well as an insightful and talented broadcaster. He was often called the "Norman Rockwell of Radio" based on his nationally-syndicated, two-minute "Straight From the Heart" features, which were heard daily on more than 100 radio stations.

The author of 19 best-selling titles, Exley now devotes his full time to writing and speaking. He currently lives with his wife Brenda Starr in a cabin on picturesque Beaver Lake in the Ozarks.